MW00945010

Logic
Course Reader

Younan

ISBN-13: 978-1503034242
ISBN-10: 1503034240

TABLE OF CONTENTS

From Nietzsche, *On Truth and Lie in an Extra-Moral Sense*, tr. Walter Kaufmann:

In some remote corner of the universe, poured out and glittering in innumerable solar systems, there once was a star on which clever animals invented knowledge. That was the highest and most mendacious minute of "world history"—yet only a minute. After nature had drawn a few breaths the star grew cold, and the clever animals had to die.

One might invent such a fable and still not have illustrated sufficiently how wretched, how shadowy and flighty, how aimless and arbitrary, the human intellect appears in nature. There have been eternities when it did not exist; and when it is done for again, nothing will have happened. For this intellect has no further mission that would lead beyond human life. It is human, rather, and only its owner and producer gives it such importance, as if the world pivoted around it. But if we could communicate with the mosquito, then we would learn that he floats through the air with the same self-importance, feeling within itself the flying center of the world. There is nothing in nature so despicable or insignificant that it cannot immediately be blown up like a bag by a slight breath of this power of knowledge; and just as every porter wants an admirer, the proudest human being, the philosopher, thinks that he sees on the eyes of the universe telescopically focused from all sides on his actions and thoughts.

It is strange that this should be the effect of the intellect, for after all it was given only as an aid to the most unfortunate, most delicate, most evanescent beings in order to hold them for a minute in existence, from which otherwise, without this gift, they would have every reason to flee as quickly as Lessing's son. [In a famous letter to Johann

Joachim Eschenburg (December 31, 1778), Lessing relates the death of his infant son, who "understood the world so well that he left it at the first opportunity."] That haughtiness which goes with knowledge and feeling, which shrouds the eyes and senses of man in a blinding fog, therefore deceives him about the value of existence by carrying in itself the most flattering evaluation of knowledge itself. Its most universal effect is deception; but even its most particular effects have something of the same character.

The intellect, as a means for the preservation of the individual, unfolds its chief powers in simulation; for this is the means by which the weaker, less robust individuals preserve themselves, since they are denied the chance of waging the struggle for existence with horns or the fangs of beasts of prey. In man this art of simulation reaches its peak: here deception, flattering, lying and cheating, talking behind the back, posing, living in borrowed splendor, being masked, the disguise of convention, acting a role before others and before oneself—in short, the constant fluttering around the single flame of vanity is so much the rule and the law that almost nothing is more incomprehensible than how an honest and pure urge for truth could make its appearance among men. They are deeply immersed in illusions and dream images; their eye glides only over the surface of things and sees "forms"; their feeling nowhere lead into truth, but contents itself with the reception of stimuli, playing, as it were, a game of blindman's buff on the backs of things. Moreover, man permits himself to be lied to at night, his life long, when he dreams, and his moral sense never even tries to prevent this—although men have been said to have overcome snoring by sheer will power.

What, indeed, does man know of himself! Can he even once perceive himself completely, laid out as if in an illuminated glass case? Does not nature keep much the most from him, even about his body, to spellbind and confine him in a proud, deceptive consciousness, far from the coils of the intestines, the quick current of the blood stream, and the involved tremors of the fibers? She threw away the key; and woe to the calamitous curiosity which might peer just once through a crack in the chamber of consciousness and look down, and sense that man rests upon the merciless, the greedy, the insatiable, the murderous, in the indifference of his ignorance—hanging in dreams, as it were, upon the back of a tiger. In view of this, whence in all the world comes the urge for truth?

Insofar as the individual wants to preserve himself against other individuals, in a natural state of affairs he employs the intellect mostly for simulation alone. But because man, out of need and boredom, wants to exist socially, herd-fashion, he requires a peace pact and he endeavors to banish at least the very crudest *bellum omni contra omnes* [war of all against all] from his world. This peace pact brings with it something that looks like the first step toward the attainment of this enigmatic urge for truth. For now that is fixed which henceforth shall be "truth"; that is, a regularly valid and obligatory designation of things is invented, and this linguistic legislation also furnishes the first laws of truth: for it is here that the contrast between truth and lie first originates. The liar uses the valid designations, the words, to make the unreal appear as real; he says, for example, "I am rich," when the word "poor" would be the correct designation of his situation. He abuses the fixed conventions by arbitrary changes or even by reversals of the names. When he does this in a self-serving way damaging to others, then society will no longer trust him but exclude him. Thereby men do not flee from being deceived as much as from being damaged by deception: what they hate at this stage is basically not the deception but the bad, hostile consequences of certain kinds of deceptions. In a similarly limited way man wants the truth: he desires the agreeable life-preserving consequences of truth, but he is indifferent to pure knowledge, which has no consequences; he is even hostile to possibly damaging and destructive truths. And, moreover, what about these conventions of language? Are they really the products of knowledge, of the sense of truth? Do the designations and the things coincide? Is language the adequate expression of all realities?

Only through forgetfulness can man ever achieve the illusion of possessing a "truth" in the sense just designated. If he does not wish to be satisfied with truth in the form of a tautology—that is, with empty shells—then he will forever buy illusions for truths. What is a word? The image of a nerve stimulus in sounds. But to infer from the nerve stimulus, a cause outside us, that is already the result of a false and unjustified application of the principle of reason...The different languages, set side by side, show that what matters with words is never the truth, never an adequate expression; else there would not be so many languages. The "thing in itself" (for that is what pure truth, without consequences, would be) is quite incomprehensible to the creators of language and not at all worth aiming for. One designates only the relations of things to man, and to express them one calls on the boldest metaphors. A nerve stimulus, first transposed into an image—first metaphor. The image, in turn, imitated by a sound—second metaphor...

Let us still give special consideration to the formation of concepts. Every word immediately becomes a concept, inasmuch as it is not intended to serve as a reminder of the unique and wholly individualized original experience to which it owes its birth, but must at the same time fit innumerable, more or less similar cases—which means, strictly speaking, never equal—in other words, a lot of unequal cases. Every concept originates through our equating what is unequal. No leaf ever wholly equals another, and the concept "leaf" is formed through an arbitrary abstraction from these individual differences, through forgetting the distinctions; and now it gives rise to the idea that in nature there might be something besides the leaves which would be "leaf"—some kind of original form after which all leaves have been woven, marked, copied, colored, curled, and painted, but by unskilled hands, so that no copy turned out to be a correct, reliable, and faithful image of the original form. We call a person "honest." Why did he act so honestly today? we ask. Our answer usually sounds like this: because of his honesty. Honesty! That is to say again: the leaf is the cause of the leaves. After all, we know nothing of an essence-like quality named "honesty"; we know only numerous individualized, and thus unequal actions, which we equate by omitting the unequal and by then calling them honest actions. In the end, we distill from them a *qualitas occulta* [hidden quality] with the name of "honesty"...

What, then, is truth? A mobile army of metaphors, metonyms, and anthropomorphisms—in short, a sum of human relations which have been enhanced, transposed, and embellished poetically and rhetorically, and which after long use seem firm, canonical, and obligatory to a people: truths are illusions about which one has forgotten that this is what they are; metaphors which are worn out and without sensuous power; coins which have lost their pictures and now matter only as metal, no longer as coins.

We still do not know where the urge for truth comes from; for as yet we have heard only of the obligation imposed by society that it should exist: to be truthful means using the customary metaphors—in moral terms: the obligation to lie according to a fixed convention, to lie herd-like in a style obligatory for all...

WHY LOGIC?

From St. Thomas Aquinas, *Commentary on the Posterior Analytics*, Preface:

As the Philosopher says in *Metaphysics* I (980b26), "the human race lives by art and reasonings." In this statement the Philosopher seems to touch upon that property whereby man differs from the other animals. For the other animals are prompted to their acts by a natural impulse, but man is directed in his actions by a judgment of reason. And this is the reason why there are various arts devoted to the ready and orderly performance of human acts. For an art seems to be nothing more than a definite and fixed procedure established by reason, whereby human acts reach their due end through appropriate means.

Now reason is not only able to direct the acts of the lower powers but is also the director of its own act: for what is peculiar to the intellective part of man is its ability to reflect upon itself. For the intellect knows itself. In like manner reason is able to reason about its own act. Therefore just as the art of building or carpentering, through which man is enabled to perform manual acts in an easy and orderly manner, arose from the fact that reason reasoned about manual acts, so in like manner an art is needed to direct the act of reasoning, so that by it a man when performing the act of reasoning might proceed in an orderly and easy manner and without error. And this art is logic, i.e., the science of reason. And it concerns reason not only because it is according to reason, for that is common to all arts, but also because it is concerned with the very act of reasoning as with its proper matter. Therefore it seems to be the art of arts, because it directs us in the act of reasoning, from which all arts proceed. Consequently one should view the parts of logic according to the diversity among the acts of reason.

Now there are three acts of reason, the first two of which belong to reason regarded as intellect. One action of the intellect is the understanding of indivisible or uncomplex things, and according to this action it conceives *what* a thing is. And this operation is called by some the informing of the intellect, or representing by means of the intellect. To this operation of the reason is ordained the doctrine which Aristotle hands down in the book of *Predicaments* (i.e., the Categories). The second operation of the intellect is its act of combining or dividing, in which the true or the false are for the first time present. And this act of reason is the subject of the doctrine which Aristotle hands down in the book entitled *On Interpretation*. But the third act of the reason is concerned with that which is peculiar to reason, namely, to advance from one thing to another in such a way that through that which is known a man comes to a knowledge of the unknown. And this act is considered in the remaining books of logic.

THE THREE ACTS OF THE INTELLECT

Act of Intellect	Focus	Product	Characteristics	Question
1. Simple Apprehension (*abstracts from senses*)	Essences or Natures	Concept/ Term	Clear or Unclear	What?
2. Judgment (*unites 2 concepts*)	Acts of Existence - "is"	Proposition	True or False	Whether?
3. Reasoning (*makes a conclusion*)	Causes or Reasons	Argument	Valid or Invalid	Why?

SIMPLE APPREHENSION - TEXTS

From Aristotle, *Posterior Analytics*, 100a4:

So out of sense-perception comes to be what we call memory, and out of frequently repeated memories of the same thing develops experience; for a number of memories constitute a single experience. From experience again – i.e. from the universal now stabilized in its entirety within the soul, the one beside the many which is a single identity within them all – originate the skill of the craftsman and the knowledge of the man of science, skill in the sphere of coming to be and the science in the sphere of being.

We conclude that these states of knowledge are neither innate in a determinate form, nor developed from other higher states of knowledge, but from sense-perception. It is like a rout in battle stopped by first one man making a stand and then another, until the original formation has been restored. The soul is so constituted as to be capable of this process.

Let us now restate the account given already, though with insufficient clearness. When one of a number of logically indiscriminable particulars has made a stand, the earliest universal is present in the soul: for though the act of sense-perception is of the particular, its content is universal – is man, for example, not the man Callias. A fresh stand is made among these rudimentary universals, and the process does not cease until the indivisible concepts, the true universals, are established: e.g. such and such a species of animal is a step towards the genus animal, which by the same process is a step towards a further generalization.

From Aristotle, *Categories* I:

Part 1

Things are said to be named 'equivocally' when, though they have a common name, the definition corresponding with the name differs for each. Thus, a real man and a figure in a picture can both lay claim to the name 'animal'; yet these are equivocally so named, for, though they have a common name, the definition corresponding with the name differs for each. For should any one define in what sense each is an animal, his definition in the one case will be appropriate to that case only.

On the other hand, things are said to be named 'univocally' which have both the name and the definition answering to the name in common. A man and an ox are both 'animal', and these are univocally so named, inasmuch as not only the name, but also the definition, is the same in both cases: for if a man should state in what sense each is an animal, the statement in the one case would be identical with that in the other.

Things are said to be named 'derivatively', which derive their name from some other name, but differ from it in termination. Thus the grammarian derives his name from the word 'grammar', and the courageous man from the word 'courage'.

Part 2

Forms of speech are either simple or composite. Examples of the latter are such expressions as 'the man runs', 'the man wins'; of the former 'man', 'ox', 'runs', 'wins'.

Of things themselves some are predicable of a subject, and are never present in a subject. Thus 'man' is predicable of the individual man, and is never present in a subject.

By being 'present in a subject' I do not mean present as parts are present in a whole, but being incapable of existence apart from the said subject.

Some things, again, are present in a subject, but are never predicable of a subject. For instance, a certain point of grammatical knowledge is present in the mind, but is not predicable of any subject; or again, a certain whiteness may be present in the body (for colour requires a material basis), yet it is never predicable of anything.

Other things, again, are both predicable of a subject and present in a subject. Thus while knowledge is present in the human mind, it is predicable of grammar.

There is, lastly, a class of things which are neither present in a subject nor predicable of a subject, such as the individual man or the individual horse. But, to speak more generally, that which is individual and has the character of a unit is never predicable of a subject. Yet in some cases there is nothing to prevent such being present in a subject. Thus a certain point of grammatical knowledge is present in a subject.

Part 3

When one thing is predicated of another, all that which is predicable of the predicate will be predicable also of the subject. Thus, 'man' is predicated of the individual man; but 'animal' is predicated of 'man'; it will, therefore, be predicable of the individual man also: for the individual man is both 'man' and 'animal'.

If genera are different and co-ordinate, their differentiae are themselves different in kind. Take as an instance the genus 'animal' and the genus 'knowledge'. 'With feet', 'two-footed', 'winged', 'aquatic', are differentiae of 'animal'; the species of knowledge are not distinguished by the same differentiae. One species of knowledge does not differ from another in being 'two-footed'.

But where one genus is subordinate to another, there is nothing to prevent their having the same differentiae: for the greater class is predicated of the lesser, so that all the differentiae of the predicate will be differentiae also of the subject.

Part 4

Expressions which are in no way composite signify substance, quantity, quality, relation, place, time, position, state, action, or affection. To sketch my meaning roughly, examples of substance are 'man' or 'the horse', of quantity, such terms as 'two cubits long' or 'three cubits long', of quality, such attributes as 'white', 'grammatical'. 'Double', 'half', 'greater', fall under the category of relation; 'in a the market place', 'in the Lyceum', under that of place; 'yesterday', 'last year', under that of time. 'Lying', 'sitting', are terms indicating position, 'shod', 'armed', state; 'to lance', 'to cauterize', action; 'to be lanced', 'to be cauterized', affection.

No one of these terms, in and by itself, involves an affirmation; it is by the combination of such terms that positive or negative statements arise. For every assertion must, as is admitted, be either true or false, whereas expressions which are not in any way composite such as 'man', 'white', 'runs', 'wins', cannot be either true or false.

Part 5

Substance, in the truest and primary and most definite sense of the word, is that which is neither predicable of a subject nor present in a subject; for instance, the individual man or horse. But in a secondary sense those things are called substances within which, as species, the primary substances are included; also those which, as genera, include the species. For instance, the individual man is included in the species 'man', and the genus to which the species belongs is 'animal'; these, therefore-that is to say, the species 'man' and the genus 'animal,-are termed secondary substances.

From Aristotle, *Topics* I.4-5:

First, then, we must see of what parts our inquiry consists. Now if we were to grasp (a) with reference to how many, and what kind of, things arguments take place, and with what materials they start, and (h) how we are to become well supplied with these, we should have sufficiently won our goal. Now the materials with which arguments start are equal in number, and are identical, with the subjects on which reasonings take place. For arguments start with 'propositions', while the subjects on which reasonings take place are 'problems'. Now every proposition and every problem indicates either a genus or a peculiarity or an accident-for the differentia too, applying as it does to a class (or genus), should be ranked together with the genus. Since, however, of what is peculiar to anything part signifies its essence, while part does not, let us divide the 'peculiar' into both the aforesaid parts, and call that part which indicates the essence a 'definition', while of the remainder let

13

us adopt the terminology which is generally current about these things, and speak of it as a 'property'. What we have said, then, makes it clear that according to our present division, the elements turn out to be four, all told, namely either property or definition or genus or accident. Do not let any one suppose us to mean that each of these enunciated by itself constitutes a proposition or problem, but only that it is from these that both problems and propositions are formed. The difference between a problem and a proposition is a difference in the turn of the phrase. For if it be put in this way, '"An animal that walks on two feet" is the definition of man, is it not?' or '"Animal" is the genus of man, is it not?' the result is a proposition: but if thus, 'Is "an animal that walks on two feet" a definition of man or no?' [or 'Is "animal" his genus or no?'] the result is a problem. Similarly too in other cases. Naturally, then, problems and propositions are equal in number: for out of every proposition you will make a problem if you change the turn of the phrase.

We must now say what are 'definition', 'property', 'genus', and 'accident'. A 'definition' is a phrase signifying a thing's essence. It is rendered in the form either of a phrase in lieu of a term, or of a phrase in lieu of another phrase; for it is sometimes possible to define the meaning of a phrase as well. People whose rendering consists of a term only, try it as they may, clearly do not render the definition of the thing in question, because a definition is always a phrase of a certain kind. One may, however, use the word 'definitory' also of such a remark as 'The "becoming" is "beautiful"', and likewise also of the question, 'Are sensation and knowledge the same or different?', for argument about definitions is mostly concerned with questions of sameness and difference. In a word we may call 'definitory' everything that falls under the same branch of inquiry as definitions; and that all the above-mentioned examples are of this character is clear on the face of them. For if we are able to argue that two things are the same or are different, we shall be well supplied by the same turn of argument with lines of attack upon their definitions as well: for when we have shown that they are not the same we shall have demolished the definition. Observe, please, that the converse of this last statement does not hold: for to show that they are the same is not enough to establish a definition. To show, however, that they are not the same is enough of itself to overthrow it.

A 'property' is a predicate which does not indicate the essence of a thing, but yet belongs to that thing alone, and is predicated convertibly of it. Thus it is a property of man to-be-capable of learning grammar: for if A be a man, then he is capable of learning grammar, and if he be capable of learning grammar, he is a man. For no one calls anything a 'property' which may possibly belong to something else, e.g. 'sleep' in the case of man, even though at a certain time it may happen to belong to him alone. That is to say, if any such thing were actually to be called a property, it will be called not a 'property' absolutely, but a 'temporary' or a 'relative' property: for 'being on the right hand side' is a temporary property, while 'two-footed' is in point of fact ascribed as a property in certain relations; e.g. it is a property of man relatively to a horse and a dog. That nothing which may belong to anything else than A is a convertible predicate of A is clear: for it does not necessarily follow that if something is asleep it is a man.

A 'genus' is what is predicated in the category of essence of a number of things exhibiting differences in kind. We should treat as predicates in the category of essence all such things as it would be appropriate to mention in reply to the question, 'What is the object before you?'; as, for example, in the case of man, if asked that question, it is appropriate to say 'He is an animal'. The question, 'Is one thing in the same genus as another or in a different one?' is also a 'generic' question; for a question of that kind as well falls under the same branch of inquiry as the genus: for having argued that 'animal' is the genus of man, and likewise also of ox, we shall have argued that they are in the same genus; whereas if we show that it is the genus of the one but not of the other, we shall have argued that these things are not in the same genus.

An 'accident' is (i) something which, though it is none of the foregoing-i.e. neither a definition nor a property nor a genus yet belongs to the thing: (something which may possibly either belong or not belong to any one and the self-same thing, as (e.g.) the 'sitting posture' may belong or not belong to some self-same thing. Likewise also 'whiteness', for there is nothing to prevent the same thing being at one time white, and at another not white. Of the definitions of accident the second is the better: for if he adopts the first, any one is bound, if he is to understand it, to know already what 'definition' and 'genus' and 'property' are, whereas the second is sufficient of itself to tell us the essential meaning of the term in question. To Accident are to be attached also all comparisons of things together, when expressed in language that is drawn in any kind of way from what happens (accidit) to be true of them; such as, for example, the question, 'Is the honourable or the expedient preferable?' and 'Is the life of virtue or the life of self-indulgence the pleasanter?', and any other problem which may happen to be phrased in terms like these. For in all such cases the question is 'to which of the two does the predicate in question happen (accidit) to belong more closely?' It is clear on the face of it that there is nothing to prevent an accident

16

from becoming a temporary or relative property. Thus the sitting posture is an accident, but will be a temporary property, whenever a man is the only person sitting, while if he be not the only one sitting, it is still a property relatively to those who are not sitting. So then, there is nothing to prevent an accident from becoming both a relative and a temporary property; but a property absolutely it will never be.

SIMPLE APPREHENSION - COMMENTARY

Intentionality - referential to another. Knowledge is *of something*.
> **First Intention** - an actual being in the world, e.g., a dog.
> **Second Intention** - a mental being, e.g., the idea of a dog.

Sign - represents another.
Signatum - the thing represented.

	Material Sign - has its own existence other than being a sign.	**Formal Sign** - is only a sign and nothing else. Only ideas.
Natural Sign - not man-made.	Smoke indicating fire.	Ideas.
Artificial Sign - man-made.	A "STOP" sign, or the word "stop."	X

Concept - an intellectual abstraction of the essence of a thing.
> **Comprehension** - the definition of the concept, e.g., "rational animal."
> **Extension** - the things to which the concept applies, e.g., "all humans."
> **Simple Concept:** "apple"
> **Complex Concept:** "green apple"
>
> **Concrete Concept:** "human"
> **Abstract Concept:** "humanity"
>
> **Collective Concept:** "All the feathers weigh 50 pounds."
> **Divisive Concept:** "Each of the feathers can be used to tickle someone."

Material Object - the actual being which is considered by the mind, e.g., "a door."
Formal Object - the aspect or part which is being considered, e.g., "the color of the door."

Term - a verbal or written expression of a concept. Conventional, i.e., agreed upon, as opposed to concepts, which are natural.

> **Subject** - the term being spoken about.
> **Predicate** - what is being said about the subject.
> **Copula** - the verb "is," which joins Subject and Predicate.

> Subject   Copula   Predicate
> The king   is   a nice guy.

> **Univocal Terms** - used in exactly the same sense:
> > "The Poodle *barks* and the Doberman *barks*."
> **Equivocal Terms** - used in totally different senses:
> > "The Doberman *barks* at the *bark* of the tree."
> **Analogical Terms** - used in similar, not identical senses:
> > "You seem *healthy*. Are eggs *healthy* for you?"

THE CATEGORIES - HOW SUBJECTS CAN BE

Substance - the nature or essence of the thing. "Man." Definition
> **Primary Substance** - the actual existing thing. "Socrates."
> **Secondary Substance** - a primary substance's nature. "Man."
Quantity - how much or how many. "Six feet tall." #
Quality - how it is - a qualification. "Tan."
Relation - how it is connected to another. "Teacher of Plato."
Action - what it is doing. "Teaching."
Passion - what is being done to it. "Being hated."
Location - where it is. "In Athens."
Position - how it is arranged. "Standing up."
Time - when it is. "A long time ago."
Possession - how it is clothed or adorned. "Wearing a toga."

Accidents exist but not part of its essence   Aspect of personal being

19

You are 6ft but not every human is 6ft.

THE PREDICABLES - HOW PREDICATES CAN BE

Genus - a broader classification. <u>"Animal."</u>
Specific Difference – what differentiates a species. <u>"Rational."</u>
Species - a stricter classification. <u>"Rational animal."</u>
Property - a non-definitive characteristic of a species. <u>"Risible."</u>
Accident - a characteristic shared by other species. <u>"Living."</u>

FORMING DEFINITIONS

Contradictory Opposition - leaves nothing out, has no overlap; <u>red and not-red</u>
Contrary Opposition - leaves things out; <u>red and white</u>

<u>**Nominal Definitions**</u> - define the **word**; 3 types:

> **Conventional Definition** - what we have agreed upon as the meaning of the word; found in dictionaries; uses synonyms:
> <u>Human</u>: any individual of the genus Homo, esp. a member of the species Homo sapiens. (dictionary.com)

> **Etymological Definition** - looks at the source of the term linguistically, based on its roots in the same or other languages:
> <u>Human</u>: c.1250, from M.Fr. humain "of or belonging to man," from L. humanus, probably related to homo (gen. hominis) "man," and to humus "earth," on notion of "earthly beings," as opposed to the gods (cf. Heb. adam "man," from adamah "ground"). (etymonline.com)

> **Stipulative Definition** - agreed upon for the sake of argument:
> <u>Human</u>: let's say for the sake of argument that a human is defined as a laughing animal.

<u>**Real Definitions**</u> - define the **thing** in its nature.

Essential Definition - genus + specific difference:
<u>Human</u> - rational animal

Descriptive Definition - (genus) + properties or accidents:
<u>Human</u> - a thing with two legs, 10 fingers, hair…

Extrinsic Cause - defines according to the thing's purpose:
<u>Hammer</u> - a thing made to hit stuff with

Material Cause - defines according to what a thing is made of:
<u>Human</u> - a bunch of water, carbon, fat, bones, etc.

Simple Apprehension – Supplement
Sometimes, Area Woman Just Feels...

theonion.com - MARCH 20, 2010 I ISSUE 46•11

BELMONT, NH—Stating that she wasn't in the best place right now, and that things have been sort of you know, Belmont resident Megan Slota announced Thursday that sometimes she just feels....

Due to a general sense of...well, it's hard to explain, the 28-year-old dental hygienist reported that she just needed to work some stuff out, and that she would probably be a little I don't know for a couple weeks or so.

"It's not anybody's fault, honestly," said Slota, standing in her kitchen and holding a mug of tea with both hands. "Sometimes I just get like this where it's like I'm not, I guess, whatever. We don't have to get into it right now."

Added Slota, "I'm really, like, argh, I don't know."

After that thing with Dave on Thursday, people were concerned that Slota was in a weird place, which she initially denied. But Slota later admitted that she was just taking some time to figure things out and needed a little space, but it's not like she wanted people to leave her alone or anything like that.

"I had a really good talk with Debra," Slota said. "She's such a good friend. It's good to know I have someone like her. It's just a crazy time right now. And I've been really busy with work, too, so that hasn't helped."

While admitting that it must suck to have to deal with her lately, Slota said that she appreciates everyone's patience while she sorts all of this stuff out. Sources close to the sort of spacey, sort of—oh gosh, what would you even call it—distracted woman confirm that it's always the same this time of year, because of her dad.

"I worry about Megan," longtime friend Alex Polson said. "Times like this, she can get a little strange. Not strange strange, but still kind of strange where you're like, 'Huh?' But you know what? She's tough. She'll get through all this and be back to her old self in no time."

Though she's been kind of blah lately, especially at the family thing where she had to be on her best behavior, friends and coworkers have been understanding about what's going on with her, and want to let her know they're there if she needs help moving, or needs someone to go shopping with her, or just wants to hang out and not talk about the thing that happened with Samantha last week.

"You know, it's like when you're just," Slota said. "You feel one way but then you're also sort of, I don't know, maybe it's just one of those things. And you don't want to force it, right? I feel like you just have to accept it sometimes, I guess."

"It is what it is," she added.

Regardless of the thing that's, oh, whatever, it'll pass eventually, Slota maintained that she's forging ahead and taking things one day at a time.

Dr. Andrei Robinson, author of the book It's, Well, I'm Not Sure How To Describe It, Really, says that Slota's condition is not uncommon. "As a therapist, I'm seeing more and more patients with problems and conditions related to Ms. Slota's," Dr. Robinson said. "But ultimately, there's not a lot I can do for them. It's just another facet of this, whatever it is. You can't understand the, you know, well, anything, really. It's all too much sometimes, but it's her deal. She's got to work through it. We've all been there, right?"

"I don't know," Dr. Robinson added. "Does that make sense?"

From Lewis Carrol's *Alice's Adventures in Wonderland*

As there seemed to be no chance of getting her hands up to her head, she tried to get her head down to them, and was delighted to find that her neck would bend about easily in any direction, like a serpent. She had just succeeded in curving it down into a graceful zigzag, and was going to dive in among the leaves, which she found to be nothing but the tops of the trees under which she had been wandering, when a sharp hiss made her draw back in a hurry: a large pigeon had flown into her face, and was beating her violently with its wings.

`Serpent!' screamed the Pigeon.

`I'm NOT a serpent!' said Alice indignantly. `Let me alone!'

`Serpent, I say again!' repeated the Pigeon, but in a more subdued tone, and added with a kind of sob, `I've tried every way, and nothing seems to suit them!'

`I haven't the least idea what you're talking about,' said Alice.

'I've tried the roots of trees, and I've tried banks, and I've tried hedges,' the Pigeon went on, without attending to her; 'but those serpents! There's no pleasing them!'

Alice was more and more puzzled, but she thought there was no use in saying anything more till the Pigeon had finished.

'As if it wasn't trouble enough hatching the eggs,' said the Pigeon; 'but I must be on the look-out for serpents night and day! Why, I haven't had a wink of sleep these three weeks!'

'I'm very sorry you've been annoyed,' said Alice, who was beginning to see its meaning.

'And just as I'd taken the highest tree in the wood,' continued the Pigeon, raising its voice to a shriek, 'and just as I was thinking I should be free of them at last, they must needs come wriggling down from the sky! Ugh, Serpent!'

'But I'm NOT a serpent, I tell you!' said Alice. 'I'm a--I'm a--'

'Well! WHAT are you?' said the Pigeon. 'I can see you're trying to invent something!'

'I--I'm a little girl,' said Alice, rather doubtfully, as she remembered the number of changes she had gone through that day.

'A likely story indeed!' said the Pigeon in a tone of the deepest contempt. 'I've seen a good many little girls in my time, but never ONE with such a neck as that! No, no! You're a serpent; and there's no use denying it. I suppose you'll be telling me next that you never tasted an egg!'

'I HAVE tasted eggs, certainly,' said Alice, who was a very truthful child; 'but little girls eat eggs quite as much as serpents do, you know.'

'I don't believe it,' said the Pigeon; 'but if they do, why then they're a kind of serpent, that's all I can say.'

This was such a new idea to Alice, that she was quite silent for a minute or two, which gave the Pigeon the opportunity of adding, `You're looking for eggs, I know THAT well enough; and what does it matter to me whether you're a little girl or a serpent?'

* * *

Then the Queen left off, quite out of breath, and said to Alice, "Have you seen the Mock Turtle yet?"
"No," said Alice. "I don't even know what a Mock Turtle is."
"It's the thing Mock Turtle Soup is made from," said the Queen.

LOGICAL FALLACIES

Fallacies of Language

Equivocation
Using a word with two different senses:
"Fire is god. Jim got fired. Therefore, Jim is god."

Amphiboly
Being unclear in syntax:
"Once I worshipped fire wearing a hat."

Accent
Being unclear in the stressed word:
"*We* didn't start the fire!" vs. "We didn't *start* the fire!" vs. "We didn't start the *fire!*"

Fallacies of Diversion

Attacking the Man (*ad hominem*)
Arguing against someone's personality instead of their argument:
"What do you mean fire is god? You're ugly."

Poisoning the Well
Pre-emptively attacking the supposed motivations of the argument:
"Whoever disagrees with the following is a traitor to the Persian empire: fire is god."

"You're Another" (*tu quoque*)
Accusing your opponent of the same mistake:
"Yes, I worship fire, but you're just as illogical as I am in worshipping water."

Genetic Fallacy
Attacks the supposed motivations of the argument:
"You only think fire is god because the Persian government told you so."

Appeal to Authority (*ad verecundiam*)
Quoting an irrelevant source as authoritative:
"Ben Affleck likes the Zoroastrian religion, so it must be true."

Appeal to Force (*ad baculum*)
Using violence to try to prove its point:
"If you don't agree with Zoroastrianism, you will be slapped in the face."

Appeal to Pity (*ad misericordiam*)
Confusing the sadness of something with a valid argument against it.
"I remember when the water-worshippers killed my father. It was devastating for me and my family. Therefore, fire is god."

Appeal to Shame (*ad ignominiam*)
Confusing the shamefulness of something with a valid argument against it.
"What do you mean you don't worship fire? Don't you realize that water-worshippers are a bunch of toothless rednecks?"

Appeal to Popularity (*ad populum;* "bandwagon fallacy")
Holding a view is correct only because many believe it:
"Everyone thinks that fire is god. It must be true."

Appeal to Ignorance (*ad ignorantiam;* "shifting the burden of proof")
Holding an implausible claim and asking the opponent to prove otherwise:
"Can you *prove* that fire is not, in fact, god?"

Fallacies of Oversimplification
Accident (*dicto simpliciter*)
Confusing substance with accident, or essence with qualification:
"Plato is different from Socrates. Socrates is a man. Therefore, Plato is not a man."

Composition and Division
Confusing a whole with a part:
"Each of the molecules in my body is microscopic. Therefore, my body is microscopic."

False Dilemma ("false dichotomy;" "The Black and White Fallacy")
Falsely limits the number of options:
"Either fire is god or water is god."

Fallacies of Argumentation
Non Sequitur ("does not follow")
Making any conclusion that is not necessary from the premises:
"My pants are green. Therefore, fire is god."

Circular Reasoning (*petitio principii*; "begging the question")
Assuming what you want to prove:
"Of course the Zoroastrian religion is true: all the Magi believe it and they're appointed by the fire god!"

Complex Question
Asking what appears to be one question which is in fact more than one:
"Have you finally admitted to yourself the truth that fire is god?"

Slippery Slope
Showing consequences to the argument that are not necessary or relevant:
"If we stop worshipping fire, the Persian empire will lose its identity, its people will be scattered, the Romans will attack us and we will all be destroyed."

Fallacies of Induction
Hasty Generalization
Making a conclusion with insufficient examples:
"Those four Persians believe that fire is god. Therefore, all Persians do."

False Cause (*post hoc ergo propter hoc*)
Claiming that something preceding something else must be its cause:
"I prayed to fire and my son got better. Therefore, the prayer healed my son."

Argument from Silence
Concluding that someone agrees or disagrees when they say nothing.
"I asked Jimmy if he believed in fire and he didn't say anything, so he must be an atheist."
"I asked Jimmy if he didn't believe in fire and he didn't say anything, so he must."

Selective Evidence
Only referring to the parts of the evidence that support your claim.
"Fire is god because it cannot be destroyed by wood, but rather destroys it" (ignoring the fact that it can be destroyed by water).

Fallacies of Procedure
Red Herring ("changing the subject")
Causing an irrelevant distraction to the argument:
"Look at how ugly those ice sculptures are. Fire must be god."

Straw Man
Setting up a false opponent; oversimplifying the opponent's position:
"So you think water is god just because it's wet? That's stupid."

JUDGMENT - TEXTS

From Aristotle, *Topics* I.7:

First of all we must define the number of senses borne by the term 'Sameness'. Sameness would be generally regarded as falling, roughly speaking, into three divisions. We generally apply the term numerically or specifically or generically-numerically in cases where there is more than one name but only one thing, e.g. 'doublet' and 'cloak'; specifically, where there is more than one thing, but they present no differences in respect of their species, as one man and another, or one horse and another: for things like this that fall under the same species are said to be 'specifically the same'. Similarly, too, those things are called generically the same which fall under the same genus, such as a horse and a man. It might appear that the sense in which water from the same spring is called 'the same water' is somehow different and unlike the senses mentioned above: but really such a case as this ought to be ranked in the same class with the things that in one way or another are called 'the same' in view of unity of species. For all such things seem to be of one family and to resemble one another. For the reaon why all water is said to be specifically the same as all other water is because of a certain likeness it bears to it, and the only difference in the case of water drawn from the same spring is this, that the likeness is more emphatic: that is why we do not distinguish it from the things that in one way or another are called 'the same' in view of unity of species. It is generally supposed that the term 'the same' is most used in a sense agreed on by every one when applied to what is numerically one. But even so, it is apt to be rendered in more than one sense; its most literal and primary use is found whenever the sameness is rendered in reference to an alternative name or definition, as when a cloak is said to be the same as a doublet, or an animal that walks on two feet is said to be the same as a man: a second sense is when it is rendered in reference to a property, as when what can acquire knowledge is called the same as a man, and what naturally travels upward the same as fire: while a third use is found when it is rendered in reference to some term drawn from Accident, as when the creature who is sitting, or who is musical, is called the same as Socrates. For all these uses mean to signify numerical unity. That what I have just said is true may be best seen where one form of appellation is substituted for another. For often when we give the order to call one of the people who are sitting down, indicating him by name, we change our description, whenever the person to whom we give the order happens not to understand us; he will, we think, understand better from some accidental feature; so we bid him call to us 'the man who is sitting' or 'who is conversing over there'-clearly supposing ourselves to be indicating the same object by its name and by its accident.

From St. Thomas Aquinas, *Commentary on On Interpretation* III.4:

The conceptions of the intellect are likenesses of things and therefore the things that are in the intellect can be considered and named in two ways: according to themselves, and according to the nature of the things of which they are likenesses. For just as a statue – say of Hercules – in itself is called and is "bronze" but as it is a likeness of Hercules is named "man," so if we consider the things that are in the intellect in themselves, there is always composition where there is truth and falsity, for they are never found in the intellect as it compares one simple concept with another. But if the composition is referred to a reality, it is sometimes called composition, sometimes division: composition when the intellect compares one concept to another as though apprehending a conjunction or identity of the things of which they are the conceptions; division, when it so compares one concept with another that it apprehends the things to be diverse. In vocal sound, therefore, affirmation is called composition inasmuch as it signifies a conjunction on the part of the thing and negation is called division inasmuch as it signifies the separation of things.

From St. Thomas Aquinas, *Commentary on On Interpretation* **III.9:**

To know this relationship of conformity is to judge that a thing is such or is not, which is to compose and divide; therefore, the intellect does not know truth except by composing and dividing through its judgment. If the judgment is in accordance with things it will be true, i.e., when the intellect judges a thing to be what it is or not to be what it is not. The judgment will be false when it is not in accordance with the thing, i.e., when it judges that what is, is not, or that what is not, is. It is evident from this that truth and falsity as it is in the one knowing and speaking is had only in composition and division.

From St. Thomas Aquinas, *Commentary on On Interpretation* **X.14, 16:**

There are, therefore, three kinds of affirmations in which something is predicated of a universal: in one, something is predicated of the universal universally, as in "every man is an animal;" in another, something is predicated of the universal particularly, as in "some man is white." The third affirmation is that in which something is predicated of the universal without a determination of universality or particularity. Enunciation of this kind is customarily called indefinite...If we add the singular to the three already mentioned there will be four modes of enunciation pertaining to quantity: universal, singular, indefinite, and particular.

JUDGMENT - COMMENTARY

Subject - what you are talking about.
Predicate - what you are saying about it.

God   is   love.   Love   is   God.
  | | vs. | |
Subject   *Predicate*   *Subject*   *Predicate*

Kinds of Propositions:
- **Categorical Proposition:** Men are pigs.
- **Compound Propositions:**
   - **Hypothetical:** If men eat ham, then men are pigs.
   - **Disjunctive:** Either men are dogs or men are pigs.
   - **Conjunctive:** Men are both dogs and pigs.

Quantity of Propositions:
- **Universal** = "<u>All</u> men are pigs"
   (**Singulars** are treated as universals: "<u>Jimmy</u> is a pig")
- **Particular** = "<u>Some</u> men are pigs"
   (includes "<u>most</u>," "<u>many</u>," etc.)

Quality of Propositions:
- **Affirmative** = "All men <u>are</u> pigs"
- **Negative** = "<u>No</u> men are pigs"

Four types of Propositions:
A - Universal Affirmative (All S is P)
E - Universal Negative (No S is P)
I - Particular Affirmative (Some S is P)
O - Particular Negative (Some S is not P)

Distribution:

A term is **distributed** when it refers to *all*;
    undistributed when it refers to *some*.

- The **Subject** of a <u>Universal</u> Proposition (A or E)
    is always distributed.
- The **Predicate** of a <u>Negative</u> Proposition (E or O)
    is always distributed.

        A - All S^d is P^u
        E - No S^d is P^d
        I - Some S^u is P^u
        O - Some S^u is not P^d

Changing Propositions:

- **Conversion** - Switch Subject and Predicate. Valid with E
    and I Propositions:
        E - No men are pigs → No pigs are men
        I - Some men are pigs → Some pigs are men

- **Obversion** - Negate the Copula and the Predicate. Valid
    with all Propositions:
        A - All men are pigs → No men are non-pigs (E)
        E - No men are pigs → All men are non-pigs (A)
        I - Some men are pigs → Some men are not non-pigs (O)
        O - Some men are not pigs → Some men are non-pigs (I)
* Note that the Proposition changes type, and that I and O
obversions are basically worthless.

Types of Opposition:

(**Opposition:** a relation between two Propositions that have
the same Subject and Predicate.)

- **Contradiction** - if one is true, the other is false, if one is
false, the other is true.
- **Contrariety** - cannot both be true, but can both be false.
- **Subcontrariety** - can both be true but cannot both be false.
- **Subalternation** - if the universal is true, then the particular
is true.
- **Superalternation** - if the particular is false, then the
universal is false.

The Square of Opposition:

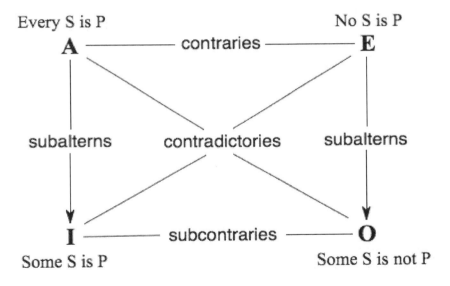

Judgment – Supplement
From Catch-22 by Joseph Heller

Private Clevinger is being accused in a private military court of making a statement about their ability to punish him. **The Colonel** *and* **Major Metcalf** *are examining the witness, and* **Lieutenant Scheisskopf** *is both prosecuting and defending attorney.*

Colonel: What did you mean when you said we couldn't punish you?

Clevinger: When, sir?

Colonel: I'm asking the questions. You're answering them.

Clevinger: Yes, sir. I –

Colonel: Did you think we brought you here to ask questions and for me to answer them?

Clevinger: No, sir. I –

Colonel: What did we bring you here for?

Clevinger: To answer questions.

Colonel: You're damned right. Now suppose you start answering some before I break your damned head. Just what the hell did you mean, you bastard, when you said we couldn't punish you?

Clevinger: I don't think I ever made that statement sir.

Colonel: Will you speak up, please? I couldn't hear you.

Clevinger: Yes, sir. I –

Metcalf: Will you speak up, please? He couldn't hear you.

Clevinger: Yes, sir. I –

Colonel: Metcalf.

Metcalf: Sir?

Colonel: Didn't I tell you to keep your stupid mouth shut?

Metcalf: Yes, sir.

Colonel: Then keep your stupid mouth shut when I tell you to keep your stupid mouth shut. Do you understand? Will you speak up, please? I couldn't hear you.

Clevinger: Yes, sir. I –

Colonel: Metcalf, is that your foot I'm stepping on?

Metcalf: No, sir. It must be Lieutenant Scheisskopf's foot.

Scheisskopf: It isn't my foot.

Metcalf: Then maybe it is my foot after all.

Colonel: Move it.

Metcalf: Yes, sir. You'll have to move your foot first, Colonel. It's on top of mine.

Colonel: Are you telling me to move my foot?

Metcalf: No, sir. Oh, no, sir.

Colonel: Then move your foot and keep your stupid mouth shut. Will you speak up, please? I still couldn't hear you.

Clevinger: Yes, sir. I said that I didn't say that you couldn't punish me.

Colonel: Just what the hell are you talking about?

Clevinger: I'm answering your question, sir.

Colonel: What question?

Scheisskopf (*from his notes*)**:** "Just what the hell did you mean, you bastard, when you said we couldn't punish you?"

Colonel: All right. Just what the hell did you mean?

Clevinger: I didn't say you couldn't punish me, sir.

Colonel: When?

Clevinger: When what, sir?

Colonel: Now you're asking me questions again.

Clevinger: I'm sorry, sir. I'm afraid I don't understand your question.

Colonel: When didn't you say we couldn't punish you? Don't you understand my question?

Clevinger: No, sir. I don't understand.

Colonel: You've just told us that. Now suppose you answer my question.

Clevinger: But how can I answer it?

Colonel: That's another question you're asking me.

Clevinger: I'm sorry, sir. But I don't know how to answer it. I never said you couldn't punish me.

Colonel: Now you're telling us when you did say it. I'm asking you to tell us when you didn't say it.

Clevinger (*takes a deep breath*)**:** I always didn't say you couldn't punish me, sir.

REASONING - TEXTS

From St. Thomas Aquinas, *Commentary on On Interpretation* **I.1:**

There is a twofold operation of the intellect, as the Philosopher says in III *De Anima*. One is the understanding of simple objects, that is, the operation by which the intellect apprehends just the essence of a thing alone; the other is the operation of composing and dividing. There is also a third operation, that of reasoning, by which reason proceeds from what is known to the investigation of things that are unknown. The first of these operations is ordered to the second, for there cannot be composition and division unless things have already been apprehended simply. The second, in turn, is ordered to the third, for clearly we must proceed from some known truth to which the intellect assents in order to have certitude about something not yet known.

From St. Thomas Aquinas, *Commentary on Posterior Analytics* **I.2:**

Since two propositions are needed for inferring a conclusion, namely, a major and a minor; when the major proposition is known, the conclusion is not yet known. Therefore, the major proposition is known before the conclusion not only in nature but in time. Further, if in the minor proposition something is introduced or employed which is contained under the universal proposition which is the major, but it is not evident that it is contained under this universal, then a knowledge of the conclusion is not yet possessed, because the truth of the minor proposition will not yet be certain. But if in the minor proposition a term is taken about which it is clear that it is contained under the universal in the major proposition, the truth of the minor proposition is clear, because that which is taken under the universal shares in the same knowledge, and so the knowledge of the conclusion is had at once.

From John of St. Thomas, *Cursus philosophicus* I.I.8.3:

A syllogism is as it were an organic instrument, which consists of the moving part and of the part moved, just as in living things one part moves another. For it is certain that the premises are the motive and the reason for knowing the conclusion, and thus the premises are necessarily and essentially required for the reason of the syllogism, from which the knowledge of the conclusion arises as if from an instrument. Similarly the conclusion itself is the object known; for the syllogism proceeds in order that the conclusion might be known through the process of inference. The syllogism is a logical tool by which the intellect is moved from one thing to another which is the object to be known, whence it should include the moving part, which constitute the premises, and the part moved, which is the inferred object or conclusion.

From St. Thomas Aquinas, *Commentary on the Ethics*, 1.1:

Order can be related to the reason in four different ways. There is an order which the reason does not make but only considers: such as the order of the things of nature. There is another order which the reason, through its own consideration, brings about in its own act, for instance, when it orders its concepts in relation to each other, and the signs of its concepts, which are significative sounds. In the third place there is the order which the reason, through its consideration, brings about in the operations of the will. In the fourth place, there is the order which the reason, through its consideration, brings about in external things of which it is the cause, e.g., an arch or a house. The order which the reason considers but does not make pertains to natural philosophy; the order which the reason brings about in its own act, through its own consideration, pertains to rational philosophy (viz. logic); the order of the acts of the will pertains to moral philosophy; the order which the reason, through its consideration, brings about in external things, pertains to mechanical arts.

REASONING - COMMENTARY

A **Syllogism** has three propositions:
two **premises** and a **conclusion**.

It contains **three terms**, each used twice:

1. The **Minor Term (S)** is the **Subject** of the **Conclusion**.
   (The **Minor Premise** is the Premise with the Minor Term)

2. The **Major Term (P)** is the **Predicate** of the **Conclusion**.
   (The **Major Premise** is the Premise with the Major Term)

3. The **Middle Term (M)** is the Term not in the Conclusion.

> All **Men** are **Mortal**. → <u>Major Premise</u>
>   M   P
>
> **Socrates** is a **man**. → <u>Minor Premise</u>
>   S   M
>
> Therefore, **Socrates** is **mortal**. → <u>Conclusion</u>
>   S   P

In order for a Conclusion to be TRUE:

- All **Terms** must be CLEAR. (*Simple Apprehension*)

- All **Propositions** must be TRUE. (*Judgment*)

- The Form of the **Syllogism** must be VALID. (*Reasoning*)

44

Checking the Validity of the Syllogism

Syllogisms have **Mood** and **Figure:**
The **Mood** is the sum of the **three "types"** of its Propositions:

All men are mortal - "A" (Universal Affirmative)
Socrates is a man - "A"
Therefore, Socrates is mortal - "A"
Mood = AAA

The **Figure** of a Syllogism is determined by the location of
the **Middle Term**:

Figure 1	Figure 2	Figure 3	Figure 4
M - P	P - M	M - P	P - M
S - M	S - M	M - S	M - S
S - P	S - P	S - P	S - P

Aristotle's Six Rules
1. A syllogism must have three and only three terms.
2. A syllogism must have three and only three propositions.
3. The middle term must be distributed at least once.
4. No term that is undistributed in the premise may be distributed in the conclusion.
5. No syllogism can have two negative premises.
6. If one premise is negative, the conclusion must be negative; if the conclusion is negative, one premise must be negative.

Corollary 1. No syllogism may have two particular premises.
Corollary 2. If a syllogism has a particular premise, it must have a particular conclusion.

REDUCTION TO FIRST FIGURE

(Figure 1) - **Barbara, Celarent, Darii, Ferio**
(Figure 2) - **Cesare, Camestres, Festino, Baroco**
(Figure 3) - **Darapti, Felapton, Disamis, Datisi, Bocardo, Ferison**

The meaning of the letters of the above names:
A, E, I, O = The **Mood** of the Syllogism
Example: Barbara = AAA Mood, **C**amestres = AEA Mood.

B, C, D, F = The type of **First Figure** Syllogism they reduce to
Example: **C**esare reduces to **C**elarent.

S, P, M, C = **What should be done** to the PREVIOUS proposition to reduce to Figure 1.
Example: Cesare - The first "E" Proposition should be Simply Converted to reduce this syllogism from Cesare (Fig. 2) to Celarent (Fig. 1). See below for Reductions.

R, L, N, T = Nothing.

Figure 1	**Figure 2**	**Figure 3**
M - P	P - M	M - P
S - M	S - M	M - S
S - P	S - P	S - P
Barbara - AAA	Cesare - EAE	Darapti - AAI
Celarent - EAE	Camestres - AEE	Felapton - EAO
Darii - AII	Festino - EIO	Disamis - IAI
Ferio - EIO	Baroco - AOO	Datisi - AII
		Bocardo - OAO
		Ferison - EIO

TYPES OF REDUCTION

S - Simple Conversion
Switch Subject and Predicate. Valid with E and I Propositions.

> *No snake is a mammal. > No mammal is a snake.*

P - Limitation (*Per Accidens*)
Switch Subject and Predicate and limit to a Particular. Valid with A Propositions.

> *Every mammal is an animal. > Some animals are mammals.*

M - Transposition (*Mutatio*)
Switch Major and Minor Premises. Never used alone.

> *Every wrestler is a tough guy.   No golfer is a tough guy.*
> *No golfer is a tough guy.   > Every wrestler is a tough guy.*
> *Therefore, no golfer is a wrestler. Therefore, no golfer is a wrestler.*

C - Contradiction (Don't worry about it)
Contradict the conclusion and switch it with the O Premise. Bocardo & Baroco. This is used only to show that one of the premises must be false.

Every animal is sensible.   Every animal is sensible.
Some stone is not sensible.   >   Every stone is an animal.
Therefore, some stone is not an animal. Therefore, every stone is sensible.

REASONING – SUPPLEMENT

WHETHER NAPS ARE NECESSARY FOR SALVATION

Thus we proceed to the only article: Whether naps are necessary for salvation.

It would seem that naps are not necessary for salvation. Salvation consists in becoming like God. God is the most actual being. Hence, we are meant to be actual beings as well. Now, naps are opposed to actuality and are hence opposed to salvation.

Also, the Apostle says, "Be watchful and awake, for your salvation is near at hand." Naps are opposed to being watchful. Hence, it follows that naps are opposed to salvation.

Furthermore, the Philosopher says that virtue consists in activity. Naps are not activity and are, therefore, not counted as virtuous. Hence, it follows that naps are opposed to salvation.

Sed contra, the Pslamist says, "He pours gifts on his beloved while they slumber." Now, salvation is a gift, and we must sleep to receive the gifts of God. Therefore, naps are necessary for salvation.

I answer that naps can be spoken of in two ways: naps in a relative sense (*secundum quid*) and naps simply speaking (*simpliciter dicta*). Secundum quid, naps are neutral in that they can be used for a good or a bad purpose. Naps, simpliciter dicta, are those naps which give us the rest that we might wake "refreshed and joyful" to praise God (as the Breviary says). To this end naps are necessary for salvation, since praising God is necessary for salvation.

Furthermore, contemplation is said to be "rest in God." Now, contemplation flows from Charity, and Charity is necessary for salvation. It follows, therefore, that naps which are also a kind of rest are necessary for salvation. Likewise, contemplation is said to be a foretaste of heavenly beatitude, so naps are a foretaste of heavenly beatitude.

Furthermore, Jesus slept in the boat. Hence, we are to sleep in the Church, for the boat is a type of the Church. We are to sleep even in church, often during homilies.

Consequently, it must be said that naps are necessary for salvation.

To the first objection, that God is the most actual being, I respond that in God's actuality is all perfection. Hence, God is actually napping.

To the second objection, that the Apostle admonishes us to be watchful, I respond that he spoke figuratively, not literally. Saint Joseph was watchful in his sleep and that is why God spoke to him in a dream. So also God spoke to many saints in dreams. Hence, we are to nap watchfully, that God might speak to us.

Finally, in response to the third objection, that the Philosopher says virtue consists in activity, I respond that the Philosopher was a pagan and cannot be expected to have understood the deep mysteries of God's napping. Had he known revelation, he would have napped much more than he did.

Sample Syllogisms

1. All things with a heartbeat are alive.
Dead men are not alive.
Therefore, dead men do not have a heartbeat.

2. All bodies are made of parts.
The soul is not made of parts.
Therefore, the soul is not a body.

3. No immaterial thing is made of parts.
Man is made of parts.
Therefore, man is not immaterial.

4. Fools are never blessed.
Some fools are lucky.
Therefore, not all lucky people are blessed.

5. No good person is skinny.
Every surfer is skinny.
Therefore, no surfer is a good person.

6. Some Detroiters carry a gun.
All Detroiters are in Michigan.
Therefore, some in Michigan carry a gun.

7. Every sailor likes to eat pizza.
Every sailor is on a ship.
Therefore, some on a ship like to eat pizza.

Non-Categorical Syllogisms

The Enthymeme:
A syllogism missing one of the propositions:

John will never get a good job because he didn't graduate.

To formulate a syllogism, find the conclusion, then the major, minor and middle terms:

Those who did not graduate will not get a good job.
John did not graduate.
Therefore, John will not get a good job.

Sorites - a series of syllogisms without conclusions.
Progressive (Aristotelian) Sorites - First premise contains the Subject:

Every man is an animal.
Every animal is a living thing.
Every living thing is a substance.
Every substance is an existing thing.
Therefore, every man is an existing.

vs.
Every man is an animal.
Every animal is a living thing.
Therefore, every man is a living thing.
etc.

Rules: Only the first premise may be particular, and only the last negative.

Regressive (Goclenian) Sorites - First premise contains the Predicate:

Every substance is an existing thing.
Every living thing is a substance.
Every animal is a living thing.
Every man is an animal.
Therefore, every man is an existing thing.

<u>Rules</u>: Only the first premise may be negative, and only the last particular.

<u>The Epicheirema</u> - a syllogism with a causal premise (a "double syllogism"):

> *Every doctor is smart because they all study hard.*
> *Lenny is a doctor.*
> *Therefore, Lenny is smart.*

This is actually two syllogisms:

> *Everyone who studies hard is smart.*
> *Doctors study hard.*
> *Therefore, doctors are smart.*
> +
> *Every doctor is smart.*
> *Lenny is a doctor.*
> *Therefore, Lenny is smart.*

Compound Syllogisms:

Conditional Syllogisms - the first proposition contains an "if...then" statement:

> *If Socrates is eating, then he exists.*
> *Socrates is eating.*
> *Therefore, Socrates exists.*

The antecedent must be affirmed or the consequent denied for the conclusion to be affected. There must be a necessary connection between antecedent and consequent.

Disjunctive Syllogisms - the first proposition contains an "either...or" statement:

Strong disjunct (cannot both be true):
> *The number 4 must be either even or odd.*
> *The number 4 is not odd.*
> *Therefore, the number 4 is even.*

Weak disjunct (both can be true):
> *Either Socrates is walking or talking.*
> *Socrates is not walking.*
> *Therefore he is talking.*

Conjunctive Syllogisms - the first proposition contains two contradictories:

> *No whole number can be both odd and even.*
> *This whole number is not even.*
> *Therefore, this whole number is odd.*

The Dilemma:

Has two "horns" either pointing to one conclusion or to two impossibilities.

> *Either A or B.*
> *If A then C.*
> *If B then C.*
> *Therefore, C.*

or:

> *Either A or B.*
> *If A then C.*
> *If B then D.*
> *Therefore either C or D.*

Ways out of a Dilemma:

1. Escaping between the horns - discovering a third possibility.
2. Taking the dilemma by the horns - denying one of the possibilities.
3. Rebutting a dilemma - comes up with a counter dilemma.

Expository Syllogisms - have a singular middle term:

> *Socrates was a philosopher.*
> *Socraes was a Greek.*
> *Therefore, a Greek was a philosopher.*

Not really a syllogism, or useful in any way.

NON-CATEGORICAL SYLLOGISMS – SUPPLEMENT

1 Corinthians 15:12-32:

Now if Christ is preached as raised from the dead, how can some of you say that there is no resurrection of the dead? But if there is no resurrection of the dead, then Christ has not been raised; if Christ has not been raised, then our preaching is in vain and your faith is in vain. We are even found to be misrepresenting God, because we testified of God that he raised Christ, whom he did not raise if it is true that the dead are not raised. For if the dead are not raised, then Christ has not been raised. If Christ has not been raised, your faith is futile and you are still in your sins. Then those also who have fallen asleep in Christ have perished. If for this life only we have hoped in Christ, we are of all men most to be pitied. But in fact Christ has been raised from the dead, the first fruits of those who have fallen asleep. For as by a man came death, by a man has come also the resurrection of the dead. For as in Adam all die, so also in Christ shall all be made alive. But each in his own order: Christ the first fruits, then at his coming those who belong to Christ. Then comes the end, when he delivers the kingdom to God the Father after destroying every rule and every authority and power. For he must reign until he has put all his enemies under his feet. The last enemy to be destroyed is death. "For God has put all things in subjection under his feet." But when it says, "All things are put in subjection under him," it is plain that he is excepted who put all things under him. When all things are subjected to him, then the Son himself will also be subjected to him who put all things under him, that God may be everything to every one. Otherwise, what do people mean by being baptized on behalf of the dead? If the dead are not raised at all, why are people baptized on their behalf? Why am I in peril every hour? I protest, brethren, by my pride in you which I have in Christ Jesus our Lord, I die every day! What do I gain if, humanly speaking, I fought with beasts at Ephesus? If the dead are not raised, "Let us eat and drink, for tomorrow we die."

From St. Thomas Aquinas, *Summa Contra Gentiles* I.15.6:

The force of Aristotle's argument lies in this: if something moves itself primarily and through itself, rather than through its parts, then insofar as it is moved it cannot depend on another. But the moving of the divisible itself, like its being, depends on its parts; it cannot therefore move itself primarily and through itself. Hence, for the truth of the inferred conclusion it is not necessary to assume as an absolute truth that a part of a being moving itself is at rest. What must rather be true is this conditional proposition: if the part were at rest, the whole would be at rest. Now, this proposition would be true even though its antecedent be impossible.

Matthew 6:22-34:

"The eye is the lamp of the body. So, if your eye is sound, your whole body will be full of light; but if your eye is not sound, your whole body will be full of darkness. If then the light in you is darkness, how great is the darkness!
"No one can serve two masters; for either he will hate the one and love the other, or he will be devoted to the one and despise the other. You cannot serve God and mammon.

"Therefore I tell you, do not be anxious about your life, what you shall eat or what you shall drink, nor about your body, what you shall put on. Is not life more than food, and the body more than clothing? Look at the birds of the air: they neither sow nor reap nor gather into barns, and yet your heavenly Father feeds them. Are you not of more value than they? And which of you by being anxious can add one cubit to his span of life? And why are you anxious about clothing? Consider the lilies of the field, how they grow; they neither toil nor spin; yet I tell you, even Solomon in all his glory was not arrayed like one of these. But if God so clothes the grass of the field, which today is alive and tomorrow is thrown into the oven, will he not much more clothe you, O men of little faith? Therefore do not be anxious, saying, `What shall we eat?' or `What shall we drink?' or `What shall we wear?' For the Gentiles seek all these things; and your heavenly Father knows that you need them all. But seek first his kingdom and his righteousness, and all these things shall be yours as well.

"Therefore do not be anxious about tomorrow, for tomorrow will be anxious for itself. Let the day's own trouble be sufficient for the day.

Sample Enthymemes

1. God does not exist because you can't find him in a test tube.

2. No one can move mountains, because mountains have no wheels.

3. Logic is boring because it's not musical.

4. I'm worth something because God loves me.

5. God loves me because I'm worth something.

6. Not all rich people are happy; some commit suicide.

7. I hate your dog because he barks at night.

8. Fred smells because he just worked out.

9. Oranges are delicious because they are citrus.

10. Guns and Roses is the greatest band ever because of Slash.

OTHER STUFF

Key for Symbolic Logic:

p, q, r, s, etc. = propositions (can be pos. or neg.)

~ = "not" (can be used with both pos. and neg. props.)

⊃ = "implies"

∴ = "therefore"

v = "or" (as in "Either…or")

& or **•** = "and"

≡ = "if and only if"

HYPOTHETICAL SYLLOGISMS
If [*antecedent*], then [*consequent*].

Pure Hypothetical Syllogisms:

If it rains, I will get wet.	$p \supset q$
If it gets wet, I will be cold.	$q \supset r$
Therefore, if it rains, I will be cold.	$\therefore p \supset r$

Valid Conditional Syllogisms:

Affirming the Antecedent (AA):

If even Socrates lacks wisdom, no man is wise.	$p \supset q$
Socrates lacks wisdom.	p
Therefore, no man is wise.	$\therefore q$

Denying the Consequent (DC):

If there is food here, I will smell it.	$p \supset q$
I don't smell it.	$\sim q$
Therefore, there is no food.	$\therefore \sim p$

Invalid Conditional Syllogisms:

Affirming the Consequent (AC):

If we are in a tornado, the house is falling apart.	p ⊃q
The house is falling apart.	q
Therefore, we are in a tornado.	∴ p

Denying the Antecedent (DA):

If we're lottery winners, we're rich.	p ⊃q
We're not lottery winners.	~p
Therefore, we're not rich.	∴ ~q

Disjunctive Syllogisms:

He is either a villain or a fool.	p v q
He's no fool.	~p
Therefore he's a villain.	∴ q

Conjunctive Syllogisms:

You cannot have your cake and eat it too.	~(p v q)
You ate your cake.	q
Therefore, you don't have it anymore.	∴ ~p

Reductio Ad Absurdum **Arguments**

Begin with the opponent's view and explore the consequences, reaching one that is absurd:

If there is no First Mover, then there are no intermediate movers. If there are no intermediate movers, there is no motion. ← *Resulting absurdity.*

INDUCTION

Induction seeks to arrive at **causes** through examining **effects.** There are different ways to describe causality:

Natural vs. Logical Causality:

Natural Causes cause the *thing*, whereas Logical Causality causes the *knowledge of the thing*.

Natural Cause - "How did he break the wall?" "He drove into it."
Logical Cause - "How do you know he broke the wall?" "He told me so."

The Four Causes:

Material – "It fell because its atoms are heavy."
Formal – "It fell because it is a bowling ball, and that's what bowling balls do."
Efficient – "It fell because I dropped it on your foot."
Final – "I dropped the bowling ball on your foot because I don't like your face."

Necessary vs. Sufficient Causality:

A Necessary Cause is *required* for the effect to occur; a Sufficient Cause is *enough alone* for the effect.

Necessary Cause – "You need to turn the key if your car is to start." (not to mention gas, oil, etc.)
Sufficient Cause – "All you need to make vinegar is some wine and some time."

Ultimate vs. Proximate Causes:

Ultimate Causes are "first" in causation (but not always in time); Proximate are "last," i.e., closer to the effect.

Ultimate/Remote/First Cause – "It was God's will that the bowling ball fell on your foot."
Proximate/Immediate/Second Cause – "It was my hand that dropped the bowling ball on your foot."

Scientific Method

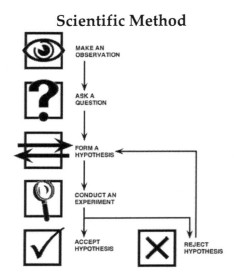

MILL'S METHODS TO DISCOVER CAUSALITY

1. Direct Method of Agreement
"If two or more instances of the phenomenon under investigation have only one circumstance in common, the circumstance in which alone all the instances agree, is the cause (or effect) of the given phenomenon."

All the people working at the power plant have cancer, and only they are, and the only difference between them and everyone else is the radiation they live with. The radiation must be causing the cancer.

2. Method of Difference
"If an instance in which the phenomenon under investigation occurs, and an instance in which it does not occur, have every circumstance in common save one, that one occurring only in the former; the circumstance in which alone the two instances differ, is the effect, or the cause, or an indispensable part of the cause, of the phenomenon."

The people working at the Springfield power plant are getting cancer, but not those in Shelbyville, but the only difference is that the Shelbyville plant workers eat White Castle. White Castle must prevent cancer.

3. Joint Method of Agreement and Difference
"If two or more instances in which the phenomenon occurs have only one circumstance in common, while two or more instances in which it does not occur have nothing in common save the absence of that circumstance: the circumstance in which alone the two sets of instances differ,

is the effect, or cause, or a necessary part of the cause, of the phenomenon."

We then gave the Springfield plant workers White Castle, and they immediately stopped getting cancer.

4. Method of Residues

"Deduct from any phenomenon such part as is known by previous inductions to be the effect of certain antecedents, and the residue of the phenomenon is the effect of the remaining antecedents."

A balloon is heavier when it is full; air must therefore have weight.

5. Method of Concomitant Variations

"Whatever phenomenon varies in any manner whenever another phenomenon varies in some particular manner, is either a cause or an effect of that phenomenon, or is connected with it through some fact of causation."

Pipe smoking is linked to longer life since statistically pipe smokers live longer than non-smokers.

ARGUMENTS FROM ANALOGY

Work better as explanations or illustrations, since they do not actually prove anything, but making something clearer to the mind can aid an argument:

Every single person whose taste I admire really loved "Shutter Island," and every single person whose taste I abhor hated it. I would probably like it.

A Fortiori **and** *A Minore* **Arguments**

Arguments from Analogy that multiply the effect by making them "all the more" and "all the less."

A Fortiori – "If you, then, who are evil, know how to give good gifts to your children, how much more will your heavenly Father give good things to those who ask him."

A Minore – "I was able to run a marathon last week. I can totally make it up these stairs."

SUMMA THEOLOGIAE I.2.1-3
ST. THOMAS AQUINAS

Article 1. Whether the existence of God is self-evident?

Objection 1. It seems that the existence of God is self-evident. Now those things are said to be self-evident to us the knowledge of which is naturally implanted in us, as we can see in regard to first principles. But as Damascene says (De Fide Orth. i, 1,3), "the knowledge of God is naturally implanted in all." Therefore the existence of God is self-evident.

Objection 2. Further, those things are said to be self-evident which are known as soon as the terms are known, which the Philosopher (1 Poster. iii) says is true of the first principles of demonstration. Thus, when the nature of a whole and of a part is known, it is at once recognized that every whole is greater than its part. But as soon as the signification of the word "God" is understood, it is at once seen that God exists. For by this word is signified that thing than which nothing greater can be conceived. But that which exists actually and mentally is greater than that which exists only mentally. Therefore, since as soon as the word "God" is understood it exists mentally, it also follows that it exists actually. Therefore the proposition "God exists" is self-evident.

Objection 3. Further, the existence of truth is self-evident. For whoever denies the existence of truth grants that truth does not exist: and, if truth does not exist, then the proposition "Truth does not exist" is true: and if there is anything true, there must be truth. But God is truth itself: "I am the way, the truth, and the life" (John 14:6) Therefore "God exists" is self-evident.

<u>On the contrary</u>, No one can mentally admit the opposite of what is self-evident; as the Philosopher (Metaph. iv, lect. vi) states concerning the first principles of demonstration. But the opposite of the proposition "God is" can be mentally admitted: "The fool said in his heart, There is no God" (Psalm 52:1). Therefore, that God exists is not self-evident.

<u>I answer that</u>, A thing can be self-evident in either of two ways: on the one hand, self-evident in itself, though not to us; on the other, self-evident in itself, and to us. A proposition is self-evident because the predicate is included in the essence of the subject, as "Man is an animal," for animal is contained in the essence of man. If, therefore the essence of the predicate and subject be known to all, the proposition will be self-evident to all; as is clear with regard to the first principles of demonstration, the terms of which are common things that no one is ignorant of, such as being and non-being, whole and part, and such like. If, however, there are some to whom the essence of the predicate and subject is unknown, the proposition will be self-evident in itself, but not to those who do not know the meaning of the predicate and subject of the proposition. Therefore, it happens, as Boethius says (Hebdom., the title of which is: "Whether all that is, is good"), "that there are some mental concepts self-evident only to the learned, as that incorporeal substances are not in space." Therefore I say that this proposition, "God exists," of itself is self-evident, for the predicate is the same as the subject, because God is His own existence as will be hereafter shown (3, 4). Now because we do not know the essence of God, the proposition is not self-

evident to us; but needs to be demonstrated by things that are more known to us, though less known in their nature — namely, by effects.

<u>Reply to Objection 1.</u> To know that God exists in a general and confused way is implanted in us by nature, inasmuch as God is man's beatitude. For man naturally desires happiness, and what is naturally desired by man must be naturally known to him. This, however, is not to know absolutely that God exists; just as to know that someone is approaching is not the same as to know that Peter is approaching, even though it is Peter who is approaching; for many there are who imagine that man's perfect good which is happiness, consists in riches, and others in pleasures, and others in something else.

<u>Reply to Objection 2.</u> Perhaps not everyone who hears this word "God" understands it to signify something than which nothing greater can be thought, seeing that some have believed God to be a body. Yet, granted that everyone understands that by this word "God" is signified something than which nothing greater can be thought, nevertheless, it does not therefore follow that he understands that what the word signifies exists actually, but only that it exists mentally. Nor can it be argued that it actually exists, unless it be admitted that there actually exists something than which nothing greater can be thought; and this precisely is not admitted by those who hold that God does not exist.

<u>Reply to Objection 3.</u> The existence of truth in general is self-evident but the existence of a Primal Truth is not self-evident to us.

Article 2. Whether it can be demonstrated that God exists?

<u>Objection 1.</u> It seems that the existence of God cannot be demonstrated. For it is an article of faith that God exists. But what is of faith cannot be demonstrated, because a demonstration produces scientific knowledge; whereas faith is of the unseen (Hebrews 11:1). Therefore it cannot be demonstrated that God exists.

<u>Objection 2.</u> Further, the essence is the middle term of demonstration. But we cannot know in what God's essence consists, but solely in what it does not consist; as Damascene says (De Fide Orth. i, 4). Therefore we cannot demonstrate that God exists.

<u>Objection 3.</u> Further, if the existence of God were demonstrated, this could only be from His effects. But His effects are not proportionate to Him, since He is infinite and His effects are finite; and between the finite and infinite there is no proportion. Therefore, since a cause cannot be demonstrated by an effect not proportionate to it, it seems that the existence of God cannot be demonstrated.

<u>On the contrary,</u> The Apostle says: "The invisible things of Him are clearly seen, being understood by the things that are made" (Romans 1:20). But this would not be unless the existence of God could be demonstrated through the things that are made; for the first thing we must know of anything is whether it exists.

<u>I answer that,</u> Demonstration can be made in two ways: One is through the cause, and is called "a priori," and this is to argue from what is prior absolutely. The other is through the

effect, and is called a demonstration "a posteriori"; this is to argue from what is prior relatively only to us. When an effect is better known to us than its cause, from the effect we proceed to the knowledge of the cause. And from every effect the existence of its proper cause can be demonstrated, so long as its effects are better known to us; because since every effect depends upon its cause, if the effect exists, the cause must pre-exist. Hence the existence of God, in so far as it is not self-evident to us, can be demonstrated from those of His effects which are known to us.

Reply to Objection 1. The existence of God and other like truths about God, which can be known by natural reason, are not articles of faith, but are preambles to the articles; for faith presupposes natural knowledge, even as grace presupposes nature, and perfection supposes something that can be perfected. Nevertheless, there is nothing to prevent a man, who cannot grasp a proof, accepting, as a matter of faith, something which in itself is capable of being scientifically known and demonstrated.

Reply to Objection 2. When the existence of a cause is demonstrated from an effect, this effect takes the place of the definition of the cause in proof of the cause's existence. This is especially the case in regard to God, because, in order to prove the existence of anything, it is necessary to accept as a middle term the meaning of the word, and not its essence, for the question of its essence follows on the question of its existence. Now the names given to God are derived from His effects; consequently, in demonstrating the existence of God from His effects, we may take for the middle term the meaning of the word "God".

<u>Reply to Objection 3.</u> From effects not proportionate to the cause no perfect knowledge of that cause can be obtained. Yet from every effect the existence of the cause can be clearly demonstrated, and so we can demonstrate the existence of God from His effects; though from them we cannot perfectly know God as He is in His essence.

Article 3. Whether God exists?

<u>Objection 1.</u> It seems that God does not exist; because if one of two contraries be infinite, the other would be altogether destroyed. But the word "God" means that He is infinite goodness. If, therefore, God existed, there would be no evil discoverable; but there is evil in the world. Therefore God does not exist.

<u>Objection 2.</u> Further, it is superfluous to suppose that what can be accounted for by a few principles has been produced by many. But it seems that everything we see in the world can be accounted for by other principles, supposing God did not exist. For all natural things can be reduced to one principle which is nature; and all voluntary things can be reduced to one principle which is human reason, or will. Therefore there is no need to suppose God's existence.

<u>On the contrary,</u> It is said in the person of God: "I am Who am." (Exodus 3:14)

<u>I answer that,</u> The existence of God can be proved in five ways.

The first and more manifest way is the argument from motion. It is certain, and evident to our senses, that in the world some things are in motion. Now whatever is in motion is put in motion by another, for nothing can be in motion except it is in potentiality to that towards which it is in motion; whereas a thing moves inasmuch as it is in act. For motion is nothing else than the reduction of something from potentiality to actuality. But nothing can be reduced from potentiality to actuality, except by something in a state of actuality. Thus that which is actually hot, as fire, makes wood, which is potentially hot, to be actually hot, and thereby moves and changes it. Now it is not possible that the same thing should be at once in actuality and potentiality in the same respect, but only in different respects. For what is actually hot cannot simultaneously be potentially hot; but it is simultaneously potentially cold. It is therefore impossible that in the same respect and in the same way a thing should be both mover and moved, i.e. that it should move itself. Therefore, whatever is in motion must be put in motion by another. If that by which it is put in motion be itself put in motion, then this also must needs be put in motion by another, and that by another again. But this cannot go on to infinity, because then there would be no first mover, and, consequently, no other mover; seeing that subsequent movers move only inasmuch as they are put in motion by the first mover; as the staff moves only because it is put in motion by the hand. Therefore it is necessary to arrive at a first mover, put in motion by no other; and this everyone understands to be God.

The second way is from the nature of the efficient cause. In the world of sense we find there is an order of efficient causes. There is no case known (neither is it, indeed, possible) in which a thing is found to be the efficient cause of itself; for so it would be prior to itself, which is impossible.

Now in efficient causes it is not possible to go on to infinity, because in all efficient causes following in order, the first is the cause of the intermediate cause, and the intermediate is the cause of the ultimate cause, whether the intermediate cause be several, or only one. Now to take away the cause is to take away the effect. Therefore, if there be no first cause among efficient causes, there will be no ultimate, nor any intermediate cause. But if in efficient causes it is possible to go on to infinity, there will be no first efficient cause, neither will there be an ultimate effect, nor any intermediate efficient causes; all of which is plainly false. Therefore it is necessary to admit a first efficient cause, to which everyone gives the name of God.

The third way is taken from possibility and necessity, and runs thus. We find in nature things that are possible to be and not to be, since they are found to be generated, and to corrupt, and consequently, they are possible to be and not to be. But it is impossible for these always to exist, for that which is possible not to be at some time is not. Therefore, if everything is possible not to be, then at one time there could have been nothing in existence. Now if this were true, even now there would be nothing in existence, because that which does not exist only begins to exist by something already existing. Therefore, if at one time nothing was in existence, it would have been impossible for anything to have begun to exist; and thus even now nothing would be in existence — which is absurd. Therefore, not all beings are merely possible, but there must exist something the existence of which is necessary. But every necessary thing either has its necessity caused by another, or not. Now it is impossible to go on to infinity in necessary things which have their necessity caused by another, as has been already proved in regard to efficient causes. Therefore we cannot but postulate the existence of some being having of itself its own necessity, and not receiving it from another, but rather causing in others their necessity. This all men speak of as God.

The fourth way is taken from the gradation to be found in things. Among beings there are some more and some less good, true, noble and the like. But "more" and "less" are predicated of different things, according as they resemble in their different ways something which is the maximum, as a thing is said to be hotter according as it more nearly resembles that which is hottest; so that there is something which is truest, something best, something noblest and, consequently, something which is uttermost being; for those things that are greatest in truth are greatest in being, as it is written in Metaph. ii. Now the maximum in any genus is the cause of all in that genus; as fire, which is the maximum heat, is the cause of all hot things. Therefore there must also be something which is to all beings the cause of their being, goodness, and every other perfection; and this we call God.

The fifth way is taken from the governance of the world. We see that things which lack intelligence, such as natural bodies, act for an end, and this is evident from their acting always, or nearly always, in the same way, so as to obtain the best result. Hence it is plain that not fortuitously, but designedly, do they achieve their end. Now whatever lacks intelligence cannot move towards an end, unless it be directed by some being endowed with knowledge and intelligence; as the arrow is shot to its mark by the archer. Therefore some intelligent being exists by whom all natural things are directed to their end; and this being we call God.

<u>Reply to Objection 1.</u> As Augustine says (Enchiridion xi): "Since God is the highest good, He would not allow any evil to exist in His works, unless His omnipotence and goodness were such as to bring good even out of evil." This is part of the infinite goodness of God, that He should allow evil to exist, and out of it produce good.

<u>Reply to Objection 2.</u> Since nature works for a determinate end under the direction of a higher agent, whatever is done by nature must needs be traced back to God, as to its first cause. So also whatever is done voluntarily must also be traced back to some higher cause other than human reason or will, since these can change or fail; for all things that are changeable and capable of defect must be traced back to an immovable and self-necessary first principle, as was shown in the body of the Article.

Hi Bree –
I've taken up vandalism these days.

Love you,

Made in the USA
Charleston, SC
10 September 2015